Dealing with Depression

GREGORY L. JANTZ, PHD

WITH ANN MCMURRAY

HENDRICKSON PUBLISHERS   ROSE PUBLISHING

Five Keys to Dealing with Depression
Copyright © 2016 Gregory L. Jantz
Aspire Press is an imprint of
Rose Publishing, LLC
P.O. Box 3473
Peabody, Massachusetts 01961-3473 USA
www.hendricksonrose.com

Printed in the United States of America
November 2017 — 3rd printing

Contents

What's Wrong *with* Me?

Sarah wondered, *What's wrong with me?* The worry, never far from her mind, intruded again. She felt rundown, listless, unable to generate energy or enthusiasm about anything. Getting up in the morning and facing each day seemed like a barrier to climb. Sometimes, she just didn't bother, choosing to mumble some vague complaint and forcing her husband to call her in sick to work. Sarah honestly couldn't remember the last time she felt fine.

Her husband was frustrated. Rejecting her early nights to bed and inexplicable lethargy, he found outside interests to expend his energies on. They orbited around each other without really connecting. Her kids seemed to handle her bystander role in the family in a similar way: passively acknowledging her, saying little, and moving ahead with their lives and activities. They moved ahead while Sarah was left behind.

Isolated from her family, Sarah ate to feel better, squeezing joy out of life through sweet, soft, and doughy comfort. Of course, the feeling-better part didn't last and required repetition. In a part of her mind, Sarah found it ironic that eating lousy was the only thing she felt motivated to do. So she kept eating and putting on weight, which made her feel even worse. She chose clothes that not only hid her shape but also matched her mood—shrouded and dark.

She just didn't care about her clothes, about her job, or even about her family, anymore. Suffocating under a blanket of her own hopelessness, Sarah felt grayed-out. She hadn't always felt this way, but that time of feeling fine was like it had occurred in someone else's life. *What's wrong with me?*

■ ■ ■

Is there a part of you that identifies with Sarah? You don't feel like yourself, but you're not exactly sure why. You're tired all the time; your body aches; you don't have energy to do much of anything. You're slowly slipping toward an edge but can't seem to stop the slide. Some days you scare yourself, because you would almost welcome falling into the abyss. What's going on?

Have you ever had a day like that? Have you ever had a week like that? Have you ever had more than a week like that? How many bad days in a row can you have before those bad days become something more? And, if something more, will that something ever get better?

Everyone feels lousy sometimes. Everyone experiences days when they just don't want to get out of bed, when they'd rather just roll over, pull the covers up over their head and call in sick to their life. Call that a bad day or just getting whacked by life; it happens to everyone.

Depression is more than an occasional whacked-by-life-and-I-don't-want-to-get-out-of-bed day. Depression is a condition marked by three characteristics: frequency, severity, and duration.

To help figure out if you're depressed, you need to ask yourself:

1. *How often does this happen? (frequency)*

2. *How bad is it when it happens? (severity)*

3. *How long does it last when it happens? (duration)*

The more it happens, the worse it is, and the longer it lasts, the more likely it is that you're not just having a bad day   you're dealing with depression.

But what exactly is depression, especially when everyone has bad days and people come in all sorts of emotional shapes and sizes? Depression is an overall category of specific feelings and behaviors. However, if you're depressed, that depression may look very different from your cousin's or aunt's or the person's down the street. Trying to compare the way you feel and matching it up with how someone else feels may not help define whether or not you are depressed.

Instead of comparing one person to another, try comparing the way you feel with the following two lists. The first I call my Yellow List, which describes symptoms that signal caution and a need to be monitored. My Red List is made up of identified symptoms of clinical depression.

Red indicators are like the stoplights at traffic intersections and railroad crossings; they need to be taken seriously and to prompt immediate action. Yellow indicators may not cause you to slam on your brakes, but they convey a message to slow down and pay attention, because, as you know, yellow can change to red.

As you look over the following Yellow List, a word of caution is needed. Some Yellows can be tricky to identify, because they may have been present in your life for a long time. You may be so used to these Yellows, they've become normal for you. A Yellow is not normal if it follows the three characteristics of depression symptoms: frequency, severity, and duration.

If you're dealing with depression, does that mean you're in a place where God cannot go? No! There is nowhere you can go physically or emotionally where God is not present.

"YOU HAVE SEARCHED ME, LORD, AND YOU KNOW ME. YOU KNOW WHEN I SIT AND WHEN I RISE; YOU PERCEIVE MY THOUGHTS FROM AFAR. WHERE CAN I GO FROM YOUR SPIRIT? YOUR RIGHT HAND WILL HOLD ME FAST."
—PSALM 139:1-2, 7, 10

YELLOW LIST

- [ ] A loss of enjoyment in established activities
- [ ] Feeling restless, tired, or unmotivated at work
- [ ] An increase in irritability or impatience
- [ ] Feeling either wound up or weighed down
- [ ] Feeling overburdened with life and its activities
- [ ] A lack of spiritual peace or well-being
- [ ] A constant anxiety or vague fear about the future
- [ ] A fear of expressing strong emotions
- [ ] Finding relief by controlling aspects of your personal behavior, including what you eat or drink
- [ ] Feeling unappreciated by others
- [ ] Feeling a sense of martyrdom, as if you are constantly asked to do the work of others
- [ ] Exercising a pattern of impulsive thinking or rash judgments

YELLOW LIST

- [ ] Apathetic when you wake up in the morning about how the day will turn out

- [ ] A sense of enjoyment at seeing the discomfort of others

- [ ] Anger at God for how you feel

- [ ] A recurrent pattern of headaches, muscle aches, and/or body pains

- [ ] Feeling left out of life

- [ ] Feeling trapped during your day by what you have to do

- [ ] Experiencing recurring gastrointestinal difficulties

- [ ] Feeling like your best days are behind you and the future doesn't hold much promise

- [ ] Displaying a pattern of pessimistic or critical comments and/or behaviors

- [ ] Bingeing on high-calorie foods to feel better

- [ ] Feeling social isolation and distancing from family or friends

YELLOW LIST

☐	Feeling that it's easier to just do things yourself instead of wanting to work with others
☐	Feeling old, discarded, or without value
☐	Feeling trapped inside your body
☐	Dreading the thought of family get-togethers or social gatherings
☐	Feeling overweight, unattractive, or unlovable
☐	Sexual difficulties or a loss of interest in sexual activities
☐	Unmotivated to try new activities, contemplate new ideas, or enter into new relationships

Living in the Yellow means diminished joy and fulfillment, yet some people seem to live in that zone for a long time, finding ways to cope until the accumulated weight of despair or a sudden, traumatic life event propels them into the Red.

RED LIST

☐	A significant change in appetite, resulting in either marked weight loss or weight gain
☐	Recurring disturbances in sleep patterns, resulting in difficulty falling and staying asleep or in sleeping too much
☐	Increased agitation or complete inability to relax
☐	Complete fatigue, overwhelming lethargy, or loss of energy
☐	Deep thoughts of sadness, despondency, despair, or loneliness, or feelings of worthlessness
☐	Inability to concentrate, focus, or make decisions
☐	Recurring thoughts of death or suicide
☐	Planning or attempting suicide

When a traumatic event happens—like a severe or chronic illness, a significant disappointment with job or family, or the illness or death of a loved one— the emotional erosion done by living in the Yellow destabilizes your ability to cope, making you more susceptible to falling into the Red of deeper depression.

I'm Depressed—Now What?

As you've looked over the Yellows and Reds, you may have concluded, *I'm depressed*. For many of you, this isn't a shock. You've known something's been very wrong for far too long, but you just haven't put a name to it. Now that "it" has the name of depression, what are you supposed to do? Won't knowing you're depressed just make you more depressed?

Interestingly, as I've worked with people over the years, I've found that many feel a sense of relief when they discover that the way they are feeling has a name. They finally have an understanding, a place. Is that place depression? Yes, but from that place, it's easier for them to articulate where they want to go. From that place, as a professional, it's easier for me to coordinate how to get them there.

I've worked with people who seemed to use up their energy just to get through the next hour or the next

God is your advocate in healing and recovery:

"HAVE I NOT COMMANDED YOU? BE STRONG AND COURAGEOUS. DO NOT BE AFRAID; DO NOT BE DISCOURAGED, FOR THE Lord YOUR GOD WILL BE WITH YOU WHEREVER YOU GO."
—JOSHUA 1:9

day. They tried a variety of prescription medications, including some that worked for a while and some that didn't really work at all.

They tried self-medicating through food, alcohol, drugs, relationships, eating disorders, self-harming, staying in bed, the Internet, Facebook—anything numbing enough to make them forget, for a time, how lousy they felt.

YOU WEREN'T MEANT TO LIVE A LIFE OF MERE SURVIVAL AND YOU DON'T NEED TO.

When depressed people are unable to pull themselves up by their mental bootstraps, so to speak, and prescribed medication or even self-medication isn't successful, life becomes a very real struggle. Instead of something worth living and enjoying, life becomes mere survival.

You can survive in the Yellows for quite a while, but that's not really living. This may seem like bad news, but actually it's good news. You weren't meant to live a life of mere survival and you don't need to—no matter how long it's been since you felt optimistic or joyful or hopeful about yourself or about life.

The Whole-Person Approach

There are five keys to overcoming depression that when integrated together provide a pathway to successful, long-term recovery. How do I know? I am privileged to watch this recovery take place in the lives of people all the time.

The five keys to overcoming depression are based on my whole-person approach to recovery. When I began my professional therapeutic career over thirty years ago, too often I saw a one-size-fits-all answer given to depressed people. They were told they had nothing to be depressed about and to "just get over it." They were told to take this or that pill and everything would be better. But they didn't get over it and everything wasn't better. They still felt lousy, still couldn't find the energy and passion to pursue their dreams, and still couldn't understand why they felt so bad in the first place. I certainly believe that medications and the power of positive thinking have their place in depression recovery, but if they are so effective, why are so many people still depressed?

This question led me to think about depression from a whole-person perspective, recognizing that a person is made up of different facets.

A whole-person is made up of five aspects:

1. Emotional

2. Intellectual

3. Relational

4. Physical

5. Spiritual

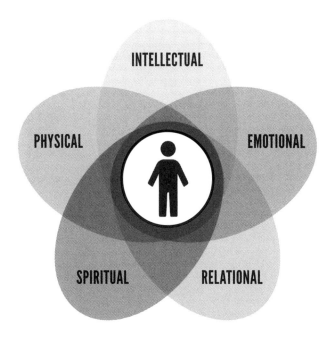

These aspects can combine for good—to promote healing and recovery—or for bad—to complicate healing and recovery. As I worked to define and refine my whole-person approach to recovery, I realized applications for a variety of mental health issues, including depression. Over thirty years later, I'm even more convinced of the value of the whole-person approach. Just as these whole-person components interact and contribute to a state of depression, these whole-person components can be addressed together to enhance recovery from depression. When they're working in harmony to reach the goal of healing from depression, recovery has more of a fighting chance at success.

KEY #1

Emotional Balance

What's wrong with me? When Mark's coworkers found out about his promotion—something he hadn't even applied for—they slapped his back, shook his hand, and gave him high fives. Mark couldn't figure out why he didn't feel that happy. When told about the new job, he'd agreed out of shock. Now he smiled back and said thanks to the congratulations, but inside he was in turmoil. What if this didn't work out? What if he couldn't do this more-important job? What if he failed? Everyone else seemed to treat his promotion like the best thing that could have happened to him. Deep down, Mark was terrified it would be the worst. Feeling slightly sick, Mark wondered if he should go home for the day.

■ ■ ■

When depression settles into a person's life, emotions become confused. A promotion at work may produce thoughts of despair and fear. Minor daily irritants can become major life hurdles. The joy of others can become a gloomy reminder of inner insecurities. When our inner thoughts are in turmoil, we have much greater difficulty navigating daily life and our emotional imbalance can tilt toward depression. The demands of life can make us angry, fearful, resentful, frustrated, and irritated. Life produces an emotional response and for some, depression becomes that response.

> The theme verse of my clinic—of my life, really—is from the book of Jeremiah:
>
> "'FOR I KNOW THE PLANS I HAVE FOR YOU,' DECLARES THE LORD, 'PLANS TO PROSPER YOU AND NOT TO HARM YOU, PLANS TO GIVE YOU HOPE AND A FUTURE.'"
> —JEREMIAH 29:11

Depressed people have lost their emotional equilibrium. All of us are born with an emotional spectrum, with the capacity to move across what we call positive and negative emotions. The positive side is exemplified by optimism, hope, and joy. The negative side can be represented by anger, fear, and guilt. Of course, there is a plethora of emotional responses in between these extremes, but I have found these positive responses and these negative responses to be the strongest at pulling people one way or the other across the emotional spectrum.

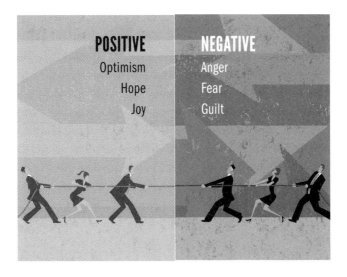

POSITIVE
Optimism
Hope
Joy

NEGATIVE
Anger
Fear
Guilt

People who are depressed live pulled to one side of the emotional spectrum—the negative side. Their emotional responses are so overrepresented by anger, fear, and guilt that they have lost the ability to absorb and experience optimism, hope, and joy. Without joy, there is no hope. Without hope, there is no optimism.

Without optimism, there is no future. People without a sense of the future become depressed.

This is not to say that anger, fear, and guilt are unnatural. If someone treats us poorly, it is natural for us to feel anger over the injustice. If we are threatened in some way, reacting in fear may save our lives. If we act badly, it is healthy for us to feel guilt. Anger can help energize us to protect and defend ourselves. Fear can motivate us to seek a solution to our danger. Guilt can produce remorse, helping us to change behavior. In proper proportion, they are healthy, appropriate emotions. We have a spectrum of emotions at our disposal to lead healthy, productive lives; and anger, fear, and guilt are on that spectrum. But like many things, too much of them is not a good thing.

Anger Out *of* Balance

Depression has been described as feeling like a suffocating blanket of apathy, a dark and heavy place that weighs down the soul. Depressed people say life seems grayed-out, as if they're numb in all their senses, except pain.

In this grayed-out, numbed-out, depression-shrouded life, anger has the power to break through. Look again at some of the yellow and red indicators of depression and notice how anger manifests itself:

INDICATORS OF DEPRESSION
☐ Anger breaks out through irritability or impatience.
☐ Anger breaks out through a sense of martyrdom when there's a feeling of being unappreciated by others.
☐ Anger fuels impulsive thinking or rash judgments.
☐ Anger shows itself through pessimistic or critical comments and/or behaviors—a negative and sarcastic response to life.
☐ Anger fuels agitation.

Anger has the capacity to break through the suffocating blanket of depression, because anger can be very empowering. Anger brings about energy and passion. But anger also makes you a target. Anger rushes you into situations for which you are not equipped, resulting in frustration and pain. Anger drowns out other responses. Anger exhausts your emotional resources.

Depressed people, who are used to that numbed-out feeling, can be surprised at how angry they really are.

In an effort to control the rage, depressed people can become emotionally anorexic. An anorexic uses the restriction of food and liquid to demonstrate an immense anger and dissatisfaction with life and with self. I've come to believe that depressed people, in a similar way, have learned to restrict the expression of emotions to demonstrate an immense anger and dissatisfaction with life and with self. A depressed person, then, is not a person devoid of emotion; a depressed person is often someone who is filled with so much strong, negative emotion that the only way to cope with feeling so bad is to try to feel nothing at all.

God cautions about living on your anger, however justified you may feel.

"MY DEAR BROTHERS AND SISTERS, TAKE NOTE OF THIS: EVERYONE SHOULD BE QUICK TO LISTEN, SLOW TO SPEAK AND SLOW TO BECOME ANGRY, BECAUSE HUMAN ANGER DOES NOT PRODUCE THE RIGHTEOUSNESS THAT GOD DESIRES."
—JAMES 1:19–20

Yet anger will not be denied. While pushed down, repressed, and unacknowledged, anger remains, festering inside. Anger vents itself in small ways: irritation at traffic, frustration with a struggling clerk, displeasure at a disobedient child, impatience with a coworker, exasperation with a spouse. The more unresolved anger a person has, the more anger builds up, venting out in random and seemingly unrelated circumstances.

Anger keeps a person in a constant state of agitation, feeling under siege. Because of this, the energy anger demands can drain a person of optimism. Optimism sees the world as, overall, a beautiful place. Anger, instead, looks at the world as a battlefield.

> "LIKE A CITY WHOSE WALLS ARE BROKEN THROUGH IS A PERSON WHO LACKS SELF-CONTROL."
> —PROVERBS 25:28
>
> "AN ANGRY PERSON STIRS UP CONFLICT, AND A HOT-TEMPERED PERSON COMMITS MANY SINS."
> —PROVERBS 29:22

Fear Out *of* Balance

Anger drains optimism, and fear steals hope, because hope is the expectation of a better tomorrow. When fear takes hold, the future is no longer something to be anticipated but something to be dreaded. Many of the indicators of depression speak to this dread: a lack of well-being, anxiety and fear about the future, feeling trapped in life.

I remember when Mark sought counseling. He was practically immobilized by the fear that his "true abilities" would be discovered and he'd be fired from his job. When Mark learned he was being promoted, he was, instead of being elated, terrified that the scrutiny of the new job would reveal weakness. Mark worried he would be "found out" and fired. Without realizing it, he began to self-sabotage the promotion. Suddenly, he couldn't seem to get projects finished. Afraid of being caught doing something wrong, Mark failed to do much of anything. He started calling in sick and felt terrible, unmotivated to even get out of bed.

Once invited in, fear is a companion that doesn't go away. Instead, fear clings to you, whispering doom in quiet moments, disrupting your sleep, and robbing you of a moment's peace. Fear says that disaster is only a

Does God know we are often afraid? Of course he does! Over seventy times in Scripture he tells us not to be afraid. Does he dismiss the circumstances that would cause us fear? No, he tells us not to be afraid, because he is with us. God-with-us changes everything!

JESUS SAID,
"PEACE I LEAVE WITH YOU;
MY PEACE I GIVE YOU. I DO
NOT GIVE YOU AS THE WORLD
GIVES. DO NOT LET YOUR
HEARTS BE TROUBLED AND
DO NOT BE AFRAID."
—JOHN 14:27

heartbeat away. Fear says there is no peace, no safety. If anger is an overwhelming emotion, fear is a jealous one. Fear seeks to co-opt positive emotions.

Guilt Out *of* Balance

Anger drains optimism, fear steals hope, and guilt crushes joy. Joy is an intensely personal pleasure, radiating from your heart and encompassing your entire being. Guilt crushes joy, because guilt says you do not deserve to have such pleasure. Guilt says what you have done or who you are means you don't deserve personal happiness.

Becky came into counseling after her mother died, with overwhelming feelings of guilt because she blamed herself for her mother's alcoholism and subsequent death from stroke. Becky felt guilt for all the trouble she gave her mother as a rebellious teenager. Her mother's complaints were especially pointed whenever the rent or utility payments were due, and her mother expected Becky to make up for her past behavior with financial support. Deep down, however, Becky knew her financial support made it possible for her mother to continue to drink heavily. After her mother died suddenly of an alcohol-related stroke, Becky became severely depressed. How could Becky justify any joy in her own life when she'd been a party to the death of her mother?

That's what guilt does. Guilt demands payment. Not only must you pay by sacrificing joy, but you must also walk around with the chains of guilt wrapped around you. Those chains are heavy—so heavy, some days you find you're unable to do anything else.

Courage *to* Recover

When a person is depressed, there are emotional roots of anger, fear, and guilt that anchor depression into a person's thinking. These roots must be uncovered, understood, and addressed in a positive, healing way. This is not a quick process. It requires time, patience, and no small amount of courage. Courage is needed to identify and acknowledge the source of anger, fear, and guilt in your life. The source of this pain may be rooted in childhood, meaning you're so accustomed to feeling this way, you may experience anger, fear, and guilt afresh at dredging up these truths. Looking at who you are and why you feel the way you do from a fresh approach can be difficult. Over the years, you've learned ways to cope with the pain, and those ways are familiar and even comforting. Giving those ways up and looking at the truth is the first step to creating change.

Some people are able to realize improvement through medication alone, but research shows there is a higher degree of healing when therapy is combined with medication.[1] Therapy or counseling provides individuals with a safe place to talk about feelings and discuss past and current events in life that have contributed to their depression. Therapists can also make suggestions about positive actions people can integrate into their lives. When I have used the whole-person approach, including an understanding of the body and the appropriate use of medication, I have found success in helping people to achieve long-term recovery and healing from depression.

It takes courage to understand the need for change. It takes courage to step out in faith and act differently. Overcoming depression

The psalmist, David, understood the crushing weight of guilt:

"MY GUILT HAS OVERWHELMED ME LIKE A BURDEN TOO HEAVY TO BEAR."
—PSALM 38:4

Yet David could also conclude:

"LORD, DO NOT FORSAKE ME; DO NOT BE FAR FROM ME, MY GOD. COME QUICKLY TO HELP ME, MY LORD AND MY SAVIOR."
—PSALM 38:21–22

requires a new paradigm because depression can't be solved by the same circumstances that created it. In order to recover, you need to change how you listen to and respond to your emotions.

Recognize, Promote, *and* Sustain

What do we do when life feels like it's piling on top of us? In depression, we bury our optimism, hope, and joy and react with anger, fear, or guilt, allowing overwhelming circumstances to knock us flat. Emotional depression can become an automatic reaction to life's trials. Reactions are automatic, but responses need not be. Depression does not have to be automatic.

Even if we may immediately react negatively, we can learn to intentionally reassert positive emotions. This may not be our first reaction, but our first reaction doesn't need to be our only response. Albert Einstein once said, "You can't solve a problem on the same level that it was created. You have to rise above it to the next level." Our reactions are on one level, but we can learn to take our responses to the next level.

The next level above automatic reaction is intentional response. You need to be intentional in your response to life and its circumstances. You need to deliberately recognize, promote, and sustain optimism, hope, and joy. In the midst of depression, the thought of sustaining even a modicum of positive feelings may appear overwhelming, a burden too heavy to bear. But aren't you already carrying around the weight of emotional baggage? Think how much energy it takes to carry around anger, fear, and guilt. When you begin to put those emotions down, you will find strength for optimism, hope, and joy.

REACTIONS ARE AUTOMATIC, BUT RESPONSES NEED NOT BE.

Negative emotions may be part of your personal landscape. If that is the case, you'll need to intentionally seek out and rediscover optimism, hope, and joy. Optimism, hope, and joy are responses that come from within you and are not necessarily derived from your outside circumstances. Regardless of the circumstances, *you* determine to remain optimistic; *you* decide to have hope; *you* derive joy.

Intentionally choosing how to respond to life is not a trivial matter; this attitude can save your life. In his book *Man's Search of Meaning*, Holocaust survivor Viktor E. Frankl set forth his answer to the question of why some people lived through the Nazi Germany concentration camps and some did not. He found that it rarely had anything to do with their physical state. Some prisoners who were extremely debilitated or ill continued to live, while some others who were in much better physical shape died. The difference, he found, was in their attitude to life. Frankl discovered that in the final analysis, strength for living is found in the ability to choose your attitude—your response—to any given situation. The situations he and others dealt with on a daily basis were deprivation, starvation, physical disease, and beatings. Yet in the midst of the hell of the concentration camp, he and others intentionally chose to respond with optimism and hope.

Frankl, who could find positives in the midst of a Nazi concentration camp, demonstrates that each of us has the opportunity to find positives in our own situations. We will not always have control over our circumstances, but we can determine to hold on to optimism, hope, and joy—to recognize them, promote them, and sustain them. This is the challenge for those who are depressed.

Negative *and* Positive Self-Talk

Each of us has a set of messages we play over and over in our minds. This internal dialogue, this personal commentary, frames how we respond to life and its circumstances.

Depression sets up a pattern of negative self-talk. Depression remembers every negative thing we've been told over the years by parents, siblings, teachers, friends, and enemies. Depression remembers every disaster, every catastrophe, every humiliation, as if it happened yesterday. These messages playing over and over in our minds fuel feelings of anger, fear, and guilt, resulting in thoughts of hopelessness.

Recovery from depression happens when a person begins to identify the source of these messages and learns to intentionally overwrite them. But the first step is identifying what those negative messages are and, often, who in your past introduced those messages.

> "FINALLY, BROTHERS AND SISTERS, WHATEVER IS TRUE, WHATEVER IS NOBLE, WHATEVER IS RIGHT, WHATEVER IS PURE, WHATEVER IS LOVELY, WHATEVER IS ADMIRABLE—IF ANYTHING IS EXCELLENT OR PRAISEWORTHY—THINK ABOUT SUCH THINGS."
> —PHILIPPIANS 4:8

For example, as a child you may have been told, "You'll never amount to anything," or "You can't do anything right." Or you may have heard something more subtle, such as, "You know you can do better," even when you knew you were trying as hard as you could. So you took in the message that you weren't good enough.

- You may feel *guilt* that you should have been good enough but weren't.

- You may feel *fear* that you aren't good enough and everyone is going to find that out.

- You may feel *anger* that you keep trying your best only to be told over and over again it isn't enough.

Negative self-talk can seem more honest, but positive self-talk is not self-deception. Rather, positive self-talk does not run from the truth but seeks to place that truth into context. For example, everyone makes mistakes. To expect perfection in yourself or anyone else is unrealistic. To expect no difficulties in life, whether through your own actions or sheer circumstance, is also unrealistic.

When negative events or mistakes happen, positive self-talk seeks to find the positive out of the negative in order to help you do better, go farther, or just keep moving forward. The practice of positive self-talk is often the process that allows you to discover the optimism, hope, and joy to be found in the situation.

Choose Your Attitude

Each of us has an array of moods we can choose from, but over time—and especially when depressed—we narrow that field down to negativity. Those who are depressed may choose to return to those negative moods that feel the most comfortable, that match how they feel and the messages they're hearing in their heads.

Mood and attitude are linked—they are interrelated but separate. Mood is how we are feeling; attitude is how we respond to the mood. We may not choose our mood, but by choosing our attitude, we go to the next level of reaction: our response. No matter what mood we initially experience, our

> "AND WE BOAST IN THE HOPE OF THE GLORY OF GOD. NOT ONLY SO, BUT WE ALSO GLORY IN OUR SUFFERINGS, BECAUSE WE KNOW THAT SUFFERING PRODUCES PERSEVERANCE; PERSEVERANCE, CHARACTER; AND CHARACTER, HOPE. AND HOPE DOES NOT PUT US TO SHAME, BECAUSE GOD'S LOVE HAS BEEN POURED OUT INTO OUR HEARTS THROUGH THE HOLY SPIRIT, WHO HAS BEEN GIVEN TO US."
> —ROMANS 5:2-5

attitude can either reinforce that mood or help us choose another.

Things happen, and each of us will have a natural reaction to those things—such as surprise or anxiety—that may be similar to the way anyone else might react.

MOOD IS HOW WE ARE FEELING; ATTITUDE IS HOW WE RESPOND TO THE MOOD.

But after our initial reaction, we have the opportunity to review that reaction and intentionally respond with a continuation of that reaction or with a more positive attitude.

When you are experiencing depression, you must work at promoting the choice of a good attitude. It can be hard work. A good attitude won't come naturally. Pessimism, negativity, sarcasm, hostility, and even apathy flow more easily when you are depressed. To overcome depression, you must turn the flow of this negative tide and strive, even if it seems like you're straining against a strong current, to promote optimism, hope, and joy.

Pessimism has a way of seeming normal. Depressed people, who live in a state of pessimism, may have difficulty recognizing that pessimism is negative. One way to discover the depth of a person's pessimism is to ask that person to give positive statements about themselves, other people, or their lives. The person may start out by saying something positive but add a negative qualifier. For example, a person may comment that his or her job is going all right but immediately add that the busy season hasn't hit yet.

It is remarkable how many times depressed people are unaware they respond in such negative ways. If the person is reminded to keep things only positive, there may be a long silence. If you are a pessimistic person, the good news is you can choose to intentionally look for the good and to respond from a positive point of view. In this case, the key to success is practice, practice, practice. Finding the bad will seem natural, and looking for the good will seem awkward. Don't be dissuaded. Keep practicing to find the positive.

Counterbalance

Emotional equilibrium comes when you learn to counterbalance anger, fear, and guilt with optimism, hope, and joy. Emotional balance is a skill you can learn and nurture in whole-person ways. This chapter has been about your emotional self; but remember, you have an intellectual self, a relational self, a physical self, and a spiritual self, all of which can be marshaled to assist your emotional self:

- Choose a positive, uplifting book and *intentionally* set aside time in your day to fill yourself up with constructive, encouraging messages. (This is your intellectual self supporting your emotional self.)

- Engage in some mild exercise this week. Physical activity is a wonderful way of promoting emotional health. Take a walk around the neighborhood. Stroll through a city park. *Intentionally* move your body and open up your focus to include the broader world around you. (This is your physical self supporting your emotional self.)

- Think of a person you really enjoy talking to—someone who makes you feel good about yourself or someone who's just fun to be around—and *intentionally* plan to spend time with that person, even if it's just for a quick chat. Make the effort to verbalize your appreciation for his or her positive presence in your life. (This is your relational self supporting your emotional self.)

- Take some time to nourish your spirit. If you are a member of a religious organization, make sure to attend services this week. If you are not, consider joining such an organization. Listen to some religious or meditative music. Spend time in quiet reflection, meditation, or prayer.

Intentionally engage in an activity that replenishes and reconnects your spirit. (This is your spiritual self supporting your emotional self.)

These actions may seem like small steps. They may even seem unachievable, given the way you feel. Please, try to do them anyway. If you are emotionally out of sync, you can't rely on how you're feeling to determine what you do. These actions, done intentionally, will help you in two ways: (1) they will assist you in focusing on optimism, hope, and joy; and (2) they will reinforce the truth that you can intentionally respond to life and its circumstances. Like Viktor Frankl, you can *choose* to respond positively. Today, choose optimism, hope, and joy.

Intellectual Integrity

Consider a single trip to the grocery store. On your list today is a new toothbrush, soda, sandwich bags, ground meat, bread, milk, eggs, margarine, and Kleenex®. Pretty standard. Should be an easy trip, right?

- There are 15 types of toothbrushes, all different colors, from extra soft to extra firm. Which is the right one?

- Regular or diet or caffeine-free or caffeine-free diet soda—and which brand?

- Sandwich bags come in 50 or 150 or 300, fold-top, single or double zipper-top.

- Ground meat is available as extra lean, lean, or regular, in varying package sizes.

- Milk can be whole, 2 percent, non-fat, skim, fat-free, enriched, in regular, soy or almond.

- Bread is plain white or honey wheat or 7-grain or 12-grain or multigrain all in different brands.

- Seven types of eggs, 10 types of margarine.

- Kleenex® comes in small square boxes or medium boxes or large rectangular ones. They could be scented or nonscented, colored or not, with lotion or not, in 100-count or 200-count boxes. Single pack or multipack.

Then when you've overcome all of those choices and make your way to the checkout, do you choose the regular line, the express line, or the self-checkout line? Paper or plastic or both? Cash, credit, or debit? Any coupons? Cash back? Need any help out? Groceries in the front seat, back seat, or trunk?

■ ■ ■

We live in a complex world that has the capacity not only to trigger our emotions but also to inundate our minds. The more we feel compelled to do, the more energy our lives require. A hurried, fast-paced life is draining. Bit by bit, detail by detail, the sheer weight of our lives can wear us down, leaving us feeling inadequate and devastated.

The pace of life can be daunting, threatening to overwhelm even the resilient. Keeping your emotional balance jumping from task to task, demand to demand, can be acrobatic even for the resilient. But what happens when you take a stressful life full of tasks and demands and add onto that a belief system that "knows" you're not good enough, that "knows" you don't deserve to be happy? Or what happens when you take that stressful life and add onto it a belief system that says happiness can only be found when you're in total control?

What You "Know"

In order to recover from depression, understanding the role of emotions is vital, but you must also understand the role of the intellect, of the mind. Recognizing what you feel is one step in the recovery process, but another step is recognizing what you know—what you believe to be true—because what you "know" may not, in fact, be the truth.

> God cautions us about what we think we know.
>
> "'FOR MY THOUGHTS ARE NOT YOUR THOUGHTS, NEITHER ARE MY WAYS YOUR WAYS,' DECLARES THE LORD."
> —ISAIAH 55:8

Let's look at the example of a half-empty glass. The truth is, yes, the glass is half empty, but is that all there is to it? If the glass is half empty, isn't it also half full? The truth of a half-empty glass is that the glass is also half full. Those people who see a half-empty glass actually see an empty glass because, to them, the glass should always be full to the brim. If the glass is not brimming, then that glass is unsatisfactory; it will always contain emptiness and loss.

No one's glass is ever truly filled all of the time. Life simply doesn't operate that way. Instead, the truth is that even a half-empty glass has fullness. Those who are depressed don't see half empty, they see completely empty. Some will rage because the glass never seems to be full. Others will despair because they are convinced they aren't worthy of even a half-empty glass. Others will quietly accept the fact that the glass will never be full for them. They look at the glass and see what isn't there instead of what is. They focus on the lack of what is absent instead of the presence of what is there.

Just because you think you know something, doesn't mean that something is true. That something could be flat-out false. That something could be partially true but lacking in full context.

In order to recover from depression, you need to strive for intellectual integrity. Integrity can be defined as adhering to a code of ethics, and that certainly is a good thing; but the integrity I mean here is a bit different. Intellectual integrity is like structural integrity. When something has structural integrity, there are no gaps or weaknesses

to create instability. When you believe something that isn't the truth or is only partially true, you leave yourself open to gaps and weaknesses that undermine intellectual integrity.

One of the keys to overcoming depression is to honestly and realistically evaluate your life and determine whether what you think you know is really the truth. As much as possible, develop a plan to accept those things that are unchangeable and a plan to change those that you can.

> The Serenity Prayer is a wonderful example of a prayer for intellectual integrity:
>
> God grant me the serenity to accept the things I cannot change, Courage to change the things I can, and Wisdom to know the difference.

Please recognize, you may be reluctant to do this for fear that it will make you even more depressed. Remaining tied to false truths and half-truths may seem more comforting that living life in the glare of intellectual honesty. If you feel that way, aren't you tired of living your life while feeling like a spectator instead of an active participant with the power to choose your own course? Unless you take intentional action, chances are that circumstances won't force a change to the positive. It's time to take control and look at where you are in your life. It's time to actively and intentionally participate in the course of your life, shoring up your intellectual integrity by understanding and accepting the truth of who you are.

- ■ If you have developed a pattern of tying self-worth to activity, you may find it difficult to let go of some of the things you are doing.

- ■ If you have developed a pattern of believing in your own incompetence, taking on new activities may frighten you with a potential for failure.

- ■ If you have developed a pattern of being afraid of making mistakes, an honest appraisal of why you are engaging in an activity may be uncomfortable, because of the needed changes it might reveal.

Press On!

In order to continue taking stock of your life, you will need to press on. Don't let any initial hesitation stop you from being honest with yourself.

Your perspective on life is based upon what you "know." These "truths" are often forged in childhood. If what you "know" is framed in negativity, your perceptions and expectations may also be negative. Another way to think of this "knowledge" is as a filter through which you view your life. Some people who seem perennially happy are said to view life through rose-colored glasses. Their filter is weighted on the side of the positive. In depression, life is viewed through gray-colored glasses. Life appears negative, oppressive, and filled with shadows.

One of the main areas that may need to be changed in order to overcome depression is what you "know" about life:

- If you "know" that life consistently treats you unfairly, then the inevitable ups and downs of life are filtered through that perception. If you "know" that life is supposed to *always* be smooth sailing, the inevitable ups and downs can cause great anxiety. Down times are not put into a proper perspective, because you don't consider them to be legitimate. Down times are supposed to happen to other people but not to you. If you're unprepared to deal with these down times, confusion, frustration, and depression can result.

- If you "know" that you don't really deserve to be happy, you will filter the events of your life to make sure you aren't. Good things will be met with suspicion, and bad things will be accepted as inevitable.

- If you "know" that the only way for you to be safe is to be in control, you will have a heightened sense of anxiety over life events. Since people are rarely in total control over their environment and never in control of other people, this "knowledge" leaves a persistent, nagging feeling of insecurity. This perpetual sense of unease can lead to anxiety and depression.

Life does not always flow smoothly. Circumstances can alter the most carefully constructed life. Traumatic events will be part of each of our lives. That we cannot change. What we can change, however, is our response to those traumatic events. If the fundamental foundation for what we know about life is based on negativity, we will have little support when bad things happen. But we can use intellectual integrity to identify and replace the false and incomplete truths we've been basing our lives on. We can replace those false and incomplete truths with a more complete understanding of ourselves, our expectations, and just what the world is truly able to offer.

Jesus illustrated this grown-up principle through a parable loved by children. "Therefore everyone who hears these words of mine and puts them into practice is like a wise man who built his house on the rock" (Matthew 7:24). The foolish man builds his house upon the sand, and when the rains and winds come, it is the foolish man's house that goes S-P-L-A-T!

Making changes in your life requires a certain level of optimism. If you find it difficult to be optimistic, consider working with a caring professional, friend, and/or spiritual counselor. Oftentimes, when the process of evaluating your life activities is done with the help of others, their vantage point offers perspectives you hadn't considered. Borrow their optimism, hope, and joy, until you are able to generate those refreshing, renewing feelings on your own.

Relational Support

Marci felt like she lived in a sort of orbital pattern with the relationships in her life. Those with whom she was in relationship, like her family, were affected by her gravitational pull. Sometimes, especially with her kids, she wasn't so sure she was pulling them in the right direction. Even though she'd been out of her childhood home for decades, she could still feel the pull from a mother who constantly expressed displeasure, a father who remained stubbornly distant, and a brother who ignored her. Like distant planets, those relationships circled around her life from afar, still pulling and tugging her in directions she didn't want to go and complicating the relationships she had now.

■ ■ ■

| Learning False Truths

A person we love or look up to has the capacity to redirect the trajectory of our lives. What they say to us becomes what we *know*, even if what they say isn't *true*. If what they say or convey is negative, how we feel about ourselves is undermined.

THE FAMILY, AND THE INDIVIDUALS IN THE FAMILY, TELLS US ABOUT OUR PLACE IN THE WORLD.

Sadly, many of us grow into adulthood with a list of childhood truths that can include many false and incomplete truths. Families, for good or ill, give us our first lessons about ourselves. We learn to view ourselves through their eyes. The family, and the individuals in the family, tells us about our place in the world. These lessons over time and into adulthood can fade from our memory, but they continue to run in the background of our lives, often without conscious notice. These are the "truths" we base our lives around, and negative ones are the background messages that can poke and prod our emotions.

People who are depressed may have picked up some of the following "truths":

LEARNED INVISIBILITY—
"If I don't want to be hurt, I shouldn't stand out."

Over the years, Scott developed a pattern of becoming "invisible" around his mother, forcing himself to merge his identity and personality into hers. What she liked, he liked. What she didn't, he didn't. If he had a different feeling or reaction, he did not express it. He came to understand that this was the tactic used by his father, who seemed to click himself off whenever Scott's mother entered the room, retreating to the television or newspaper. Scott continued this pattern by aligning himself with other, more dominant, personalities as an adult, living his life hiding in the shadows, anxious and depressed.

LEARNED HELPLESSNESS—
"Bad things happen, but they're never my fault."

Susan grew up in a family of victims. Nothing bad that ever happened in her family was considered to be their fault. If a bill was late, the post office was to blame. If the car broke down, the mechanic was to blame. If a job was lost, the economy was to blame. Employers were never fair. Workers never did the job right. Teachers were biased. Neighbors were mean.

Susan learned to externalize blame for every bad thing in her life. She perceived herself as powerless to control the bad things that happened. All she could do was complain about what befell her, including being depressed. She went from professional to professional, trying to find a "fix." She felt even more victimized when she found fault with every solution offered.

LEARNED WORTHLESSNESS—
"What I do is never enough."

Tim's father let his opinion be known early and often that Tim would never amount to much. If he did well in school, he still wasn't smart enough. If he excelled in sports, he could always be better. If he did well in business, he still wasn't savvy enough. His father's high standards had a way of creeping up, tantalizingly out of reach.

Tim's father may have written Tim off, but Tim didn't write his father off. Instead, Tim developed a pattern of demanding perfection. Only through perfection could he hope to obtain his father's blessing. Tim stubbornly refused to believe that his father had no intention of giving his approval.

LEARNED IMPATIENCE—
"I am in control of what happens to me."

At fifty-two years of age, Amy was used to controlling her life. As the head of a department in a major company, Amy gave orders and expected immediate results. She told people how high to jump, and they did. Those who didn't measure up to Amy's level of expectation didn't last long. Amy was finally at a place in her life where she felt like everything was working the way it was supposed to—her way. Then she suffered a major health crisis. Amy felt betrayed by her body, and each physical setback pushed her closer to the edge of depression. She was afraid that if she didn't recover her physical strength soon, she never would.

Amy relied upon a pattern of pushing through life's challenges, using her intellect and forceful personality. These were things she'd always counted on. These were things her family had taught her. Make a decision. Fix whatever was broken and move on. Amy was supposed to be in control of what happened to her. The reality of Amy's recuperation was not living up to this perception, which she found deeply disturbing. If she couldn't count on this, what could she count on?

The intentions of adults may not be to pass along negative messages to children, yet that is often what happens. Children tend to mirror what they see around them, good or bad. Without ever being told, children may develop a working model for life influenced by the suspicion, insecurity, perfectionism, self-centeredness, frustration, or oppressive behavior of influential adults. This model produces feelings of worthlessness, helplessness, and hopelessness, all of which suffocate optimism, hope, and joy.

You may have a background where negativity or even abuse was evident in your family. Or you may look back at your childhood and conclude your family can't be a source of your depression, because you don't remember any negative or abusive experiences.

As much as parents and adults try to minimize the damage done to their children through their own mistakes and faulty behaviors, it is not possible to completely eliminate negative influences. A careless comment or unkind remark can be enough to plant in a child's mind a seed that grows into a false perception.

Well-meaning adults can make mistakes where children are concerned, such as what happened in Mark 10: "People were bringing little children to Jesus for him to place his hands on them, but the disciples rebuked them. When Jesus saw this, he was indignant. He said to them, 'Let the little children come to me, and do not hinder them, for the kingdom of God belongs to such as these'" (13–14).

By their actions, the disciples conveyed the perception that children were not important to Jesus, when the opposite was true! Perhaps this is a perception you received growing up—that God loved you but was really too busy to be bothered by you. These are types of perceptions that become false truths.

Dealing *with* False Perceptions

Search Your Past

A search through your past is not meant to assign blame;
it is, rather, a mature look at your family to discover
what might contribute to depression. It is so important
for you to be able to identify the burdens from past
relationships that may be slowing down your rate of
recovery. Think about the members of your immediate
family—parents, siblings, and grandparents. Think
about how you relate to each of these family members
and what you learned about yourself from them:

- How did they treat you?

- What were some ways
  they hurt you?

- What were some ways
  they made you feel
  valuable and special?

Most likely, your experi-
ences with your family will
be a mixed bag of good
and bad, positive and
negative, uplifting and
deflating. As you're

ferreting out the negative, don't forget to think about positive things you learned. Remember that the negative responses may come easier than the positive ones. Be patient and allow the positive ones to come up to the surface as well.

Examine the Present

As you review past relationships, take some time to examine your current relationships. Many times, our present relationships are a direct reflection of the quality and content of our past relationships. If your childhood experience is predominantly negative, you may feel more comfortable in the same type of relationship as an adult. For example, a child with alcoholic parents will often be drawn to an alcoholic spouse. A child growing up with an overbearing parent will often choose to marry the same sort of person. We seek the familiar, even if that familiar is negative.

An unfortunate fact of human nature is that we often emulate the very patterns we dislike. If you have several negative relationships, you will want to examine your own role to see if you are the common negative denominator. If you are, then choosing to be more positive has the power to change the orbital dynamics of all of your relationships.

Realizing the ties your family may have to depression can be very painful. You may need to accept a painful reality about your upbringing. You may find yourself reliving pain. You may need to give up who you wanted to be as a child, so you can accept who you are now. This is a significant transition. Understanding the benefits can make this transition easier. As you redefine your family relationships, the insight and understanding you gain will assist you in strengthening all of your relationships—from your family of origin to your current family, from good friends to casual acquaintances, from business contacts to coworkers.

THE MOST FUNDAMENTAL RELATIONSHIP YOU HAVE IS WITH YOURSELF.

Evaluate Your Self-Talk

Perhaps the most fundamental relationship you have is with yourself. Though you interact with others, you are in constant communication with yourself through self-talk. This inner dialogue sets the stage for how you react to life. This inner dialogue can either help or hinder your ability to intentionally respond to life.

If your self-talk is out of balance—either magnifying or minimizing your role in each day's events—your ability to maintain a healthy relationship with yourself is compromised. When you magnify yourself, you become a victim to your own perfectionism. When you minimize yourself, you become a captive to your own mistakes.

There is great value in acknowledging and affirming the truth. Having the courage to accept and integrate the truth builds self-esteem. Life-affirming self-talk allows you to recognize the truth. Whenever you're empty of life-affirming self-talk, turn to life-affirming God-talk.

Your past and present relationships have molded your personality, and these personality traits will invariably enter into future relationships. Think about how you talk to yourself. Listen to how you talk to you; then listen to how you talk to others. Often, our conversations with others are reflections of the conversations we have with ourselves.

Set Your Boundaries

Sometimes, we are in relationships with extremely negative people. Sadly, these individuals can be family members who feel they have a right to act as an emotional, physical, or financial drain on our lives.

If you continue in these relationships, your ability to overcome depression can be seriously compromised. When a relationship contributes to a state of depression, it is time to change that relationship for your own health and well-being.

If this person is a member of your family, it may not be possible for you to completely cut off contact. Wherever possible, you should attempt to mend this relationship, hopeful of change from the other person. If you have tried to mend the relationship and have made the changes you feel you are able to make, yet it still remains a significant drain on your optimism, hope, and joy, then you will need to modify the boundaries of that relationship.

> Forgiveness is difficult but so necessary.
>
> JESUS TOLD US, "DO NOT JUDGE, AND YOU WILL NOT BE JUDGED. DO NOT CONDEMN, AND YOU WILL NOT BE CONDEMNED. FORGIVE, AND YOU WILL BE FORGIVEN."
> —LUKE 6:37

You will need to interact with that person less and assert yourself more. You will need to decide under what conditions you are able to continue with this relationship and then communicate these boundaries. It will be up to the other person to decide whether or not he or she can continue in relationship with you under those conditions. If this person refuses to accept your boundaries and wishes to continue with the destructive status quo, you must withdraw from the relationship until the other person modifies his or her behavior toward you and respects the boundaries you have set.

Communicating these boundaries should not be done in a confrontational manner. Boundaries should be stated in a natural, matter-of-fact way. You do not need to apologize or feel guilty about setting boundaries; they are normal and healthy for all relationships.

Take Steps to Forgive

As you move forward in your recovery from depression, don't forget the role of forgiveness. If you are thinking of the forgiveness you need, move beyond the guilt and condemnation. As you consider the forgiveness you need to extend to others, release the blame, anger, and resentment. You control who and what you forgive.

> "BE KIND AND COMPASSIONATE TO ONE ANOTHER, FORGIVING EACH OTHER, JUST AS IN CHRIST GOD FORGAVE YOU."
> —EPHESIANS 4:32

Take steps to forgive, so you can mend existing relationships, modify damaging relationships, and strengthen affirming relationships. You will then be well positioned to create new ones, which is a wonderful hope for the future.

Physical Healing

Feeling depressed is not just a mental state. Depression is a debilitating whole-body condition that must be addressed physically as well as mentally. The whole-person approach accepts the body as a complex organism and looks for systemic reasons for depression. As Dr. Robert A. Anderson, founding president of the American Holistic Medical Association, says: "A definitive diagnosis of depression should not be made until physical conditions have been surveyed."[2]

The body is not merely along for the ride into depression. The body is an active participant, with the capacity to aggravate or improve symptoms of depression. The first stop on the road to recovery from depression for many people is a physician's office. After all, they *feel* bad. Whatever the factors leading to their depression, many will attempt to obtain a medical diagnosis for physical symptoms.

There are studies showing that addressing physical conditions can have a dramatic effect in overcoming depression. Psychiatrist Richard Hall has found "evidence [of] dramatic and complete clearing of psychiatric symptoms when medical treatment for underlying physical disorders was instituted."[3]

The body holds its own special key to overcoming depression. Physical illnesses as well as physical conditions that may not be diagnosed or readily apparent can contribute to depression. Yet even when blood work and medical examinations are done, the physical culprits involved in depression can be overlooked. Like a detective, you need to be informed and persistent to discover the truth. To begin, let's examine several known contributors to depression.

Medical *and* Health Conditions

■ HYPOGLYCEMIA

Mary came to *The Center* suffering from anxiety and depression. Her moods swung from hopelessness and lethargy to being stressed out and anxious. She was terrified she was bipolar because of her roller-coaster moods. Mary wasn't bipolar, but she was hypoglycemic, which triggered her depression and anxiety.

Over the course of her adult life, Mary developed a pattern of hypoglycemia based upon her eating habits and food choices. She preferred quick, calorie-rich foods eaten sporadically, with large amounts of caffeine throughout the day. The caffeine and sweets propelled her headlong into nervousness and anxiety as her blood sugar levels spiked. The resulting crash of insulin brought feelings of depression and physical depletion. At these low times, Mary doubted her abilities, fretted over her age, and raged over any mistake. Her body was playing right into her fears of unworthiness and inadequacy to handle her job.

THE BODY HOLDS ITS OWN SPECIAL KEY TO OVERCOMING DEPRESSION.

Hypoglycemia can cause weakness, mental dullness, confusion, and fatigue. All of these symptoms, when taken together, can exacerbate depression.

■ HEART DISEASE

Research has shown that one out of every five people who suffer a heart attack will become depressed. Conversely, a link between depression and heart disease was found in a study at the Johns Hopkins School of Hygiene and Public Health, which reported that depressed people were four times more likely to have a heart attack than people who were not depressed. It has been speculated that such an attack might result from a weakened immune system due to the stress hormones secreted during bouts of depression. It's also possible that depressed people might be neglecting themselves or not taking their medications properly. Often the reduction of

blood flow and circulation that occurs with heart disease can cause a loss of physical vitality, which may be interpreted as depression.

■ ANEMIA

Anemia is a condition in which the blood lacks iron. Symptoms of anemia, similar to depression, include fatigue, weakness, and lethargy. It is difficult to experience mental alertness, optimism, or energy when your body is physically run down. Women have a much higher incidence of anemia.

■ SLEEP APNEA

Sleep apnea is a condition where the air passages in the throat close off during sleep. It is more common in those who are overweight and older, as the muscles in the throat lose rigidity and become limp upon relaxation. Those who suffer from sleep apnea fluctuate between gasping and suffocating. This pattern severely strains the body and makes getting a good night's sleep impossible. The resulting symptoms are fatigue, mental confusion, and lethargy—all associated with a state of depression.

■ DIABETES

Diabetes is the body's inability to regulate its own blood sugar. The constant up-and-down stress of elevated versus low blood sugar levels can compromise the body's ability to regulate important nutrient absorption and hormonal levels, which provide protection from depressive mood swings.

■ SEASONAL AFFECTIVE DISORDER (SAD)

This depressive cycle—also known as the winter blues—is tied to the body's secretion of melatonin, a hormone that regulates the body's biological clock and coordinates the sleep-wake cycle. SAD sufferers experience periods of moderate to intense depression during the winter.

■ HEREDITY

Depression appears to run in families. Half of manic-depressives have at least one parent who also has the disorder, and a study of twins showed that identical twins were twice as likely to share depression as fraternal twins. Educate yourself on the health background of your family, especially of parents or siblings who have experienced depression, whether clinically diagnosed or not. If immediate family members are no longer alive, talk to relatives.

■ DEHYDRATION

Most people don't drink enough water. When the body is hydrated, toxic substances are flushed out of the system. Dehydration impairs the body's ability to perform vital functions, causing fatigue, weakness, dizziness, and mental dullness. Caffeinated and alcoholic beverages promote dehydration, making the condition worse.

■ ENDOCRINE DISORDERS

Research shows that most patients with hypothyroidism, or a thyroid deficiency, have symptoms consistent with clinical depression.[4] When the endocrine system (comprised of the thyroid and adrenal glands) is not working properly, depression has been a result.

■ PUBERTY

The onset of puberty in both girls and boys can result in depression. Puberty is a time of transition, physically and emotionally. The combination of societal and physical factors is potent and can be overwhelming to young people emerging from childhood into adulthood.

■ POSTPARTUM DEPRESSION

Also known as "the baby blues." Many new mothers experience mild depression after the birth of a child, due to the drop of estrogen and progesterone levels after delivery, with symptoms usually fading within a week. Studies indicate that if a woman has a history of depression prior to pregnancy, she is at a higher risk for developing postpartum depression.

■ PREMENSTRUAL SYNDROME

This syndrome is increasingly linked to certain depressive symptoms: despondent mood, irritability, exhaustion, and bouts of crying. If you are a woman, you will want to be aware of how your monthly cycle coincides with your feelings of depression.

■ MENOPAUSAL PHASES

During menopause, the body produces less estrogen, progesterone, and testosterone—all vital hormones. Progesterone and testosterone production can decrease at a faster rate than estrogen, upsetting the proper balance and causing estrogen dominance. With this imbalance, mood changes can occur and depression may result. These hormonal fluctuations can also affect the operation of the thyroid gland, causing hypothyroidism (discussed above).

■ LOW TESTOSTERONE

During the natural aging process in men, testosterone production is decreased. Higher testosterone levels are known to produce vitality, lean muscle mass, lower body fat, and enhanced sexual performance. The lowering or loss of these functions can produce depression in men as they age. This impacts the physical as well as psychological changes in men. One study found a significant link between low testosterone and depression in older men.[5]

■ ALLERGIES AND SENSITIVITIES

A food allergy or sensitivity can arise from an over-consumption of certain foods. Eaten over and over, day in and day out, the body can build up intolerance to them, resulting in sensitivity or an allergic reaction. Research has revealed a link between depression and allergies. In one study, 70 percent of patients with a diagnosis of depression reported having a history of allergy.[6]

The good news is that when an allergy is discovered and alleviated, often the feelings of depression lift. Psychiatrist Dr. Abram Hoffer puts it this way: "When one is relieved, so is the other. Treatment of the allergy will then, in most cases, cure the depression. I've seen this in several hundred patients over the past years and I can no longer doubt this conclusion."[7]

■ YEASTS

A majority of those I treat for eating disorders have experienced recurrent yeast infections. As these yeast infections are treated, physical energy improves, insatiable cravings decrease, and depressive symptoms are remarkably lightened.

It is normal to find some yeast in the digestive tract, where it lives in balance with healthy digestive bacteria. However, there are situations where the population of healthy bacteria is diminished, allowing the yeast—especially a one-celled yeast called *Candida albicans*—to overproduce. Yeast feeds on sugar, so the more yeast in your system, the more your body will crave sugar. As the yeast feeds on sugar, it produces toxins as a by-product.

One of these toxins is ethanol, a known central nervous system depressant. When such toxins are dumped into your system, the body must work overtime to flush them out. Overgrowth of yeast in the small intestine interferes with protein digestion and amino acid absorption. In addition, the toxicity of the yeast can cause the body to become allergic to foods it tolerated before.

Yeasts can weaken the lining of the digestive wall so that food substances can actually leak into the blood stream before being fully digested (leaky gut syndrome). As the body works overtime to fight off this leakage, fatigue and a general loss of vitality result. Yeast overgrowth can also be a factor in chronic fatigue syndrome.

■ MULTIPLE CHEMICAL SENSITIVITY

There are certain people who have a heightened sensitivity to such chemicals as perfumes, deodorants, cleaning products, solvents—the list goes on and on. Our culture is awash in chemicals, and some people have an extremely low tolerance for them. For those individuals, any one of the following might happen:

- A woman's perfume at church can produce a migraine headache.

- A man's cigar in a crowd can lead to nausea.

- The cleaning solution used in the grocery store can lead to muscle pain.

Too often, these suffering individuals are considered hypochondriacs by those around them. In pain, confused about the source, fearful that it might just be all in their heads, these individuals can plummet into depression.

Environmental Factors

■ LEAD

Lead is a natural by-product of our industrialized society. As a heavy metal, lead is toxic to the body in large doses. Toxic levels can enter our bodies over time through small amounts stored in the body's fat cells. A depressed mental state can occur from lead poisoning. Lead is found in the following:

- *Eating ware*—Under-fired pottery can contain large amounts of lead, especially if produced non-professionally or imported from countries with low environmental standards. Lead crystal is also something to be wary of.

- *Older plumbing fixtures*—Lead was often used in older plumbing and piping. Water that stands in those pipes will absorb lead and contaminate drinking water.

- *Lead-soldered food cans*—These food cans have a rougher seam than non-lead-soldered cans, which have a smooth seam or a rounded bottom.

- *Paint*—From the 1950's or earlier, paint was routinely made with lead. Even if that older, contaminated paint has been covered over, any sanding or scraping can create lead-filled dust, which can be inhaled or absorbed through the skin.

- *Some Asian medications*—Certain medications prepared by traditional Asian methods can contain toxic levels of mercury, arsenic, and lead.[8]

■ ALUMINUM

Aluminum can cause depressive symptoms and is found in or can develop in a wide variety of ways: in antacids; through dialysis[9]; from cookware; in tap water in some cities with outdated water treatment facilities; aluminum salts in foods, like processed cheese, spices, and baking powder; some antiperspirants and deodorants; old appliances, like corroded air conditioners or aluminum-core water heaters.

■ MERCURY

Mercury poisoning can produce depression and can be found in dental fillings; over-the-counter pharmaceuticals containing thimerosal or sodium ethyl mercury (in certain antiseptics, ointments, cosmetics, laxatives, eyedrops, contraceptive gels, and douches); broken equipment, such as fluorescent lighting, thermometers, and certain scientific equipment; household products, such as fabric softeners, floor polishes, wood preservatives, adhesives, fungicides, paints, dyes, tattoos, and fabrics; fish products—some seafood absorb and store high concentrations of mercury found in their environment, like tuna, swordfish, shellfish, and seaweed; occupational exposure—those who routinely work with mercury, such as dentists or dental personnel, embalmers, photographers, painters, and those working around batteries or pressure gauges.

■ ORGANIC SOLVENTS

Organic solvents are found everywhere, but the most troubling are those that are petrochemical based. Petrochemical-based solvents are found in everything from the pen you write with to perfumes, glues, motor oil, and cleaning products.

According to *Dealing with Depression Naturally* by Syd Baumel, "at the Centers for Disease Control and elsewhere, researchers have repeatedly found an abnormal degree of depression, irritability, mental impairment, and other symptoms of so-called 'painters' syndrome' in persons chronically exposed to acceptable occupational levels of VOS [volatile organic solvents]."[10]

Self-Induced Substances

■ ALCOHOL

A known depressant, alcohol is a mood-altering drug and is toxic to the body in large doses. Alcohol also promotes dehydration.

■ TOBACCO

A known depressant, tobacco has a sedative-like effect on its users, which is why cigarettes are a major drug of choice for many people.

■ CAFFEINE

Many people utilize caffeine as a stimulant. However, if you ingest over 500 milligrams of caffeine per day, the opposite effect can occur. Too much caffeine acts as a depressant, causing fatigue. This is especially true when caffeine is combined with tobacco.

■ BIRTH CONTROL PILLS

Oral contraceptives impair the conversion of nutrients into serotonin by the body, affecting mood and sleep.

■ ANTIBIOTICS

Bacteria-killing medications also kill healthy bacteria, especially in our digestive tract, leaving the way open for the proliferation of unhealthy bacteria and yeasts. An overabundance of

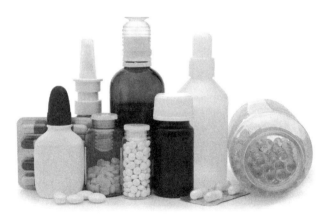

unhealthy bacteria in our digestive tracts inhibit our ability to absorb essential B-vitamins and important digestive-assisting enzymes.

■ ANTIHISTAMINES

Over-the-counter allergy medications can cause fatigue, lethargy, and mental dullness, mirroring feelings of depression.

■ CERTAIN MEDICATIONS

There are currently over two hundred medications on the market that have been shown to have the potential to cause depression (this possible side effect is usually listed in the medication's fine print). These include certain blood pressure medications, drugs used to treat Parkinson's disease, diet pills, arthritis medications, ulcer medications, and seizure medications. Even medications used primarily as tranquilizers, such as Valium and Halcion, have been shown to cause depression under certain conditions.[11]

Your body is a remarkable, complex system with an amazing ability to heal. It is also a finely tuned instrument that can be stressed out of balance by factors listed here.

You should already be tracking how and what you eat. Take a tour of where you live and evaluate your surroundings. What substances are part of your day? Include personal care products and household cleaning products. Check under sinks and in laundry areas. Look in medicine cabinets and on your bathroom counter. Track all of the chemicals in your home. These are the chemicals you expose yourself to on a regular basis. Be sure to include all soaps, cleaners, aerosols, and sprays. What is in use by other people in your home? Just because you are not using a product does not mean you are not being exposed to it.

Do you have carpets? Allergists will tell you that carpets are one of the first things to get rid of if you are experiencing heightened allergies at home. Carpets are repositories of all kinds of bacteria, mold, mildew, allergens, and pests. They also have been known to contain chemical substances, such as adhesives and formaldehyde.

PHYSICAL CONTRIBUTORS TO DEPRESSION

Medical and Health Conditions:

- [ ] Hypoglycemia
- [ ] Heart Disease
- [ ] Anemia
- [ ] Sleep Apnea
- [ ] Diabetes
- [ ] Seasonal Affective Disorder (SAD)
- [ ] Heredity
- [ ] Dehydration
- [ ] Endocrine Disorders
- [ ] Puberty
- [ ] Postpartum Depression
- [ ] Premenstrual Syndrome
- [ ] Menopausal Phases
- [ ] Low Testosterone
- [ ] Allergies and Sensitivities
- [ ] Yeasts
- [ ] Multiple Chemical Sensitivity

Environmental Factors:

- [ ] **LEAD:** lead-soldered cans, under-fired pottery, old plumbing fixtures, lead paint, some Asian medications

- ☐ **ALUMINUM:** antacids, dialysis, cookware, some tap water, aluminum salts in foods (processed cheese, spices, baking power), antiperspirants and deodorants, old appliances.
- ☐ **MERCURY:** dental fillings, pharmaceuticals containing thimerosal or sodium ethyl mercury, broken equipment (fluorescent lighting, thermometers, scientific equipment), household products (fabric softeners, floor polishes, wood preservatives, adhesives), fungicides, paints, dyes, tattoos, fabrics, some fish products, occupations such as dental personnel, embalmers, photographers, painters, and those working around batteries and pressure gauges
- ☐ **ORGANIC SOLVENTS:** petrochemical-based products in perfumes, glues, motor oil, cleaning products

Self-Induced Substances:

- ☐ Alcohol
- ☐ Tobacco
- ☐ Birth Control Pills
- ☐ Antihistamines
- ☐ Caffeine
- ☐ Antibiotics
- ☐ Certain Medications

The Good News

While the number of potential factors in physical depression is large, the good news is a small number of positive changes can bring about enormous benefit. Over the years, I've been able to identify five lifestyle choices you can make that will dramatically improve your health. They are not complicated and are based in age-old common sense:

1. **HEALTHY EATING**
2. **NUTRITIONAL SUPPORT**
3. **PROPER HYDRATION**
4. **PHYSICAL MOVEMENT**
5. **RESTFUL SLEEP**

1. HEALTHY EATING

Healthy eating means choosing as many whole, unprocessed foods as possible:

- Fresh fruits and vegetables
- Dairy products (eggs, milk, butter, cream, cheese)
- Whole grains
- Legumes (beans)
- Lean meats, fish, poultry
- Nuts
- Oils (especially flaxseed and olive oil)

Eating healthy is not only what and where you eat but also how you eat, so keep the following in mind as you make whole-food choices:

- *Don't eat too much.* Stop eating before you actually feel full. Intentionally start out with smaller portions and wait a few minutes before deciding if you need more.

- *Eat a variety of whole foods.* Healthy eating is not limited eating; rather, it is intentional eating that encompasses a medley of choices. Remember, produce is more than just apples and lettuce. Many times our choices are dictated by what we are used to, what we grew up with. Be adventurous and try different whole foods.

- *Choose a healthy ratio of food.* Eat more fruits and vegetables than breads. Eat more breads than dairy products. Eat more dairy products than meat and poultry. Eat more meat and poultry than sugars and fats. Choose healthy fats, such as those rich in omega-3s, and avoid trans fatty acids and saturated fats.

Daniel rejected the rich food and wine at the royal table, in exchange for vegetables and water. The king's steward was fearful that Daniel and his friends would look worse than those who ate the king's food. But that did not happen:

"AT THE END OF THE TEN DAYS, THEY LOOKED HEALTHIER AND BETTER NOURISHED THAN ANY OF THE YOUNG MEN WHO ATE THE ROYAL FOOD."
—DANIEL 1:15

Depressive thinking is tied to reactive thinking. Eating patterns can also be reactive. Just as recognizing, promoting, and sustaining optimism, hope, and joy are intentional choices, so is eating healthy. One supports the other. It is empowering to know that you can choose everything you put in your mouth. In overcoming depression, you want to make each bite count.

2. NUTRITIONAL SUPPORT

Eating healthy is a wonderful beginning, but overcoming depression will require the additional nutritional step of supplementation. There are four categories of supplements important to good health in general and in overcoming depression specifically:

- Vitamins
- Minerals
- Amino acids
- Essential fatty acids

Deficiencies in these substances have been clinically shown to produce symptoms of depression. There are specific tests that can determine what your levels of various nutrients are. These can be ordered through a certified nutritionist, registered dietitian, or physician. Naturopathic physicians can be an excellent source of help because these doctors are specially trained to integrate nutritional strategies into wellness.

3. PROPER HYDRATION

Most people don't drink enough water. Experts disagree on what constitutes enough, but most of them agree, we're not drinking as much water as we should. Rather than try to nail down "enough" to a specific amount of water for every person, I tend to have people check their own bodies for adequate hydration. How do you do that? Check your urine. If your urine is routinely dark yellow, you're not drinking enough. Your body is well hydrated when your urine is a light yellow or even clear.

I recommend keeping a BPA-free water bottle with you at all times. If you find water boring, you can flavor your water with pieces of fruit. Find the way you like your water best and keep at it, increasing your consumption by eight ounces at a time until your body says you're getting enough.

A word of caution, however, is needed: it is possible to drink too much water and dilute important nutrients in the body, like potassium. If in doubt, check with your primary care physician about the range of hydration right for you.

4. PHYSICAL MOTION

Rob came to me tired, burned out, and overweight, due to his high-stress, sedentary lifestyle. He sat at home. He sat at work. He sat in the car. He sat and watched television, with a remote in his hand. The more he sat, the larger and the more unhappy and unhealthy he became.

When I first broached the subject of exercise, Rob laughed and said he considered exercise a four-letter word. Besides, every time he had tried to exercise in the past, he had failed. "Then, don't exercise," I suggested. "Just move more."

No matter what you call it, physical motion is vital to a healthy life. It is also effective in relieving depression. The *British Journal of Sports Medicine* reported that walking thirty minutes each day alleviated symptoms of depression more quickly than many pharmaceutical antidepressants.[12] A Duke University study found that those who exercised were four times more likely to remain depression-free six months after the start of treatment than those who took medication. [13]

Like Rob, many of you may have difficulty imagining exercise as part of your life. You may have visions of gigantic weight lifters or slender long-distance runners and conclude you were never meant to be an athlete. Healthy movement is not defined merely by athletic competition. Rather, it is starting from wherever you are and gradually adding more motion. Keep in mind the following principles:

- **START SLOW.** By starting slow, you give your body a chance to catch up to your mental decision to begin moving more.

- **PICK YOUR MOTION.** Try walking, low-impact aerobics, swimming, or modifying a favorite activity, such as golf (choosing to walk part of the way instead of riding in the cart).

- **MAINTAIN CONSISTENCY.** Physical motion needs to become a life choice. It's not about the next few weeks or the next few months or the next few years. It's about establishing a routine, a ritual if you will, of being good to yourself through movement.

- **FIND A FRIEND.** If you find motivating yourself to exercise a challenge, ask someone to join you. Personal interaction, as well as physical movement, is of tremendous value. You may soon find that you are going farther and doing more than you ever imagined, because you are concentrating more on the other person than on the exercise.

- **BE PREPARED FOR ACHES.** While it is important to start out slow, you don't want to stay so slow that you're not accomplishing anything physically. Ideally, you want to be able to work into an exercise routine that will produce a light sweat. Sweat is one of the main ways the body detoxifies itself.

- **WATCH OUT FOR PAIN.** While aches are to be tolerated, be aware of any pain. Pain is the body's signal that something is wrong. If it has been a while since you've engaged in any physical activity, consider going to your primary care physician and obtaining a physical examination. Ask his or her guidance in planning the type, duration, and frequency of an exercise.

 ## 5. RESTFUL SLEEP

Depression interferes with the healthy production and operation of serotonin and melatonin—neurotransmitters utilized for the body's sleep-wake cycle. As you work toward recovery, you will want to assist your body in any way you can to achieve restful sleep:

- **GIVE YOURSELF ENOUGH TIME TO GET ADEQUATE REST.** Eight hours, granted, is an average, but five to six hours a night is probably not going to provide what you need.

- **ESTABLISH A SET TIME TO GO TO BED EVERY NIGHT.** Studies show that it is far better for your sleep cycle to go to bed and get up each day at approximately the same time. This applies to weekends as well as weekdays.

- **INTENTIONALLY PREPARE FOR REST.** Try reading for enjoyment, listening to soothing music or nature sounds, or quietly meditating.

- **CUT OUT CAFFEINE IN THE LATE AFTERNOON AND EVENING HOURS.** Caffeine is a stimulant and can interfere with your body's ability to know when it is actually tired. Instead of drinking coffee or caffeinated soda at dinner, drink water or herbal tea.

- **REDUCE THE ACTIVITY, NOISE, AND LIGHT LEVELS AS YOU GO INTO THE EVENING HOURS.** Start turning off lights, turning down volumes, and putting away electronics as the evening progresses.

- **AVOID EATING LATER IN THE EVENING.** Your body cannot fully rest if your digestive system stays up late to process your ten o'clock snack.

> PSALM 4:8 PROMISES, "IN PEACE I WILL BOTH LIE DOWN AND SLEEP, FOR YOU ALONE, LORD, MAKE ME DWELL IN SAFETY."

You can integrate each of these five lifestyle choices individually and collectively as a way to fortify your body against the ravages of depression.

KEY #5:

Spiritual Support

Taylor grew up believing in God, even when she was ridiculed by others. She and God were supposed to have a deal: she would believe in him and he would make sure her life was good. When Taylor became depressed, she considered herself abandoned by God. Where was the fruit of the Spirit spoken of in Galatians 5:22? This sense of betrayal haunted her too-many sleepless nights and invaded her thoughts. If Taylor couldn't count on God, who was left?

Disappointment turned to anger. Taylor prayed to get over her depression, but God didn't fix her. Why not? Taylor began to doubt God's love for her. She started to feel singled out. She knew John 3:16—"For God so loved the world . . ."—but concluded that God had a lousy way of showing his love, at least to her.

■ ■ ■

Have you picked up the stream of thought in Taylor's line of reasoning? It takes snippets of truth—God loves you, and Christians are to live a life of joy—and twists those around into something meant to injure, not give comfort. This line of reasoning was not from God; this was Taylor's depression talking, and depression is a deceiver!

Spiritual Questions

Who am I? Why am I here? What is my purpose? These are deeply personal questions that I, as a Christian, believe are also deeply spiritual. These are questions most people wrestle with over the course of their lives.

DEPRESSION IS A DECEIVER!

By answering these questions, people come to accept their own identities, understand their value in the world, and define a purpose worth striving for.

Depression distorts those questions and blocks healthy answers. Depression instead asks: Where is joy? When will this be over? Why is this happening?

How did I get this way? The answers depression provides weaken a person's belief in life and the future. Depression says you are alone in your misery. Depression says nothing is ever going to get better. Depression says you're not worth anything. In contrast, faith strengthens a person's belief in life and the future. Faith argues that you are not alone, and faith assures that there is a Father who values and loves you.

When life doesn't seem worth living, when there doesn't seem any truth or joy or even answers in the world, the spiritual connection of faith provides a source of truth, joy, and answers outside of you. This spiritual reservoir can spring up and replenish parched souls.

When you are in the midst of depression, you must stop listening to the voice of depression and concentrate on God's truths:

■ **GOD DOES LOVE YOU.**

> *"For God so loved the world that he gave his one and only Son, that whoever believes in him shall not perish but have eternal life."*—John 3:16

■ GOD WANTS YOU TO EXPERIENCE JOY.

"Gladness and joy will overtake them, and sorrow and sighing will flee away." —Isaiah 51:11

■ THROUGH GOD'S STRENGTH, YOU CAN LEARN AND GROW EACH DAY.

"It is God who arms me with strength and keeps my way secure." —2 Samuel 22:33

■ GOD'S DESIRE IS FOR YOU TO KNOW CONTENTMENT IN LIFE.

"I have learned the secret of being content in any and every situation." —Philippians 4:12

■ WITH GOD'S HELP, YOU CAN RESPOND TO YOUR CIRCUMSTANCES INSTEAD OF REACT.

"Do not conform to the pattern of this world, but be transformed by the renewing of your mind. Then you will be able to test and approve what God's will is—his good, pleasing and perfect will." —Romans 12:2

■ GOD WANTS YOU TO LOOK FORWARD TO TOMORROW.

"Because of the Lord's great love we are not consumed, for his compassions never fail. They are new every morning; great is your faithfulness." —Lamentations 3:22–23

God-Talk

How do you fill your life and your mind with God-talk? The Bible is full of life-affirming messages. As good as these affirmations are, however, they must be supported by action. Positive self-talk and an acknowledgment of God-talk are done intentionally, even if you don't feel like it. Affirmations are action based, not emotion driven. You must be able to understand and act out your knowledge of the role of love and joy in your life, even if at any given moment you do not feel joyful or lovable. How you feel about a truth does not alter its validity.

LISTEN TO GOD INSTEAD OF YOUR DESPAIR.

In the midst of your depression, listen to God instead of your despair. Fill your mind with promises and hope from his Word. Always measure against the truth in Scripture what you are told by any religious group. And don't let others tell you what the Bible says; read it for yourself. There are reasons for your depression, but God's desiring you to be unhappy and miserable is not one of them.

Forgive

You may blame yourself for decisions and actions you've made that contributed to your state of depression. You may be so hard on yourself for past mistakes that your depression sometimes feels like relief, that you are finally getting what you deserve.

You may blame others for the way their decisions or actions have hurt you and contributed to your depression. You may blame others for simply not doing enough to help you or for being too wrapped up in their own problems to know you were hurting.

AS YOU LEARN TO FORGIVE OTHERS, IT BECOMES EASIER TO FORGIVE YOURSELF.

On the road to recovery, blame is a dead end masquerading as a shortcut. Forgiveness, on the other hand, can appear to be a much longer, more difficult road to take. But when you blame another person or circumstances, you turn power over to that person or circumstance. Forgiveness returns power to you and allows you to respond, not merely react. Forgiving others has another helpful benefit: as you learn to forgive others, it becomes easier to forgive yourself.

Learn

Even amidst the fiery trial of depression, God is able to bless you and help you to grow. You must decide to meet him in this challenge for your life and to learn more about him. Through difficult struggles, you learn about your true nature. You learn who makes up your true network of support. As you are comforted and supported, you learn about the steadfast love of the Lord.

Trust

Recovery from depression is not put on hold until you have everything figured out. Some of the reasons for your depression will be evident, and some you may never completely understand. You don't have to wait until all the reasons are evident. Deeply buried answers take time to come to the surface, and God reveals truth in his own time. Have faith. Rely on Proverbs 3:5–6, which says, "Trust in the LORD with all your heart and lean not on your own understanding; in all your ways submit to him, and he will make your paths straight." Trust in the Lord, even when he seems far off, and he will help guide you out of your depression.

Obey

There will be times when you do not want to forgive or learn or trust. After the gray of depression, the real world can seem bright and loud; it can hurt, like coming out of a dark building into the sunlight. You may not want to come out, but God does want you to. At that point, you must do what God wants and not what you want.

Hope

In the midst of depression, hope may be the hardest to practice. Yet hope whispers the surety of a better tomorrow. It is as fragile as a dream and as strong as a promise. Hope is the bedrock of your recovery from depression. Hang on to hope and it will not disappoint you. That is a promise from God: "Those who hope in me will not be disappointed" (Isaiah 49:23). Joy and peace are found in recovery from depression. They are not a daydream but a solid promise from a loving God. They are promised as you surrender yourself—and your depression—to him.

| Faith *and* Belief

We are creatures of flesh and blood, but we are also spirit. Faith and belief in yourself and in your recovery are important for success. Depression is not merely an emotional upheaval or a physical condition; depression is also a spiritual assault on the truth of God's love, the promise of his care and concern, and his desire for you to experience an abundant life.

BELIEF AND FAITH ARE TWIN ANCHORS

Faith is complete trust or confidence, and belief is an acceptance that something is true. Faith may be seen as heart knowledge, whereas belief may be seen as head knowledge. Belief and faith are twin anchors when the mundane threatens to drag you down. When you don't feel like loving yourself, God still does. When you don't feel you are worthy of recovery, Christ demonstrates your worth through his death. When you don't have the strength to continue, God offers his Spirit.

Spiritual Support

The following are some positive steps you can take to gain spiritual support for your recovery:

- If you don't already have a Bible, I encourage you to get one, and pick a theme verse for your recovery. Look in the concordance in the back of the Bible and search for verses with certain key words like "hope," "joy," or "peace." Make sure your choice reflects the way God feels about you, not the way you feel about yourself. If you have trouble finding a theme verse, you might try Mark 9:23–24: "Everything is possible for the one who believes. ... Help me overcome my unbelief!" Memorize your verse and use it to keep focused on recovery.

- If you already have a Bible you use consistently, I encourage you to try a different version. Sometimes, reading over a verse with a different word or phrasing can open up new meanings. Try reading the same verse or passage from a different translation (or two).

- If you are not attending a religious service, make plans to start attending one. Look in the newspaper or make calls to religious services in the area that interest you. If you already attend services, recommit to going each week, and take the time necessary to prepare yourself spiritually for the worship experience.

■ Keep a journal of your prayers. If you are unfamiliar with prayer, consider utilizing the ACTS method:

● *Adoration* to God

● *Confession* of sins

● *Thanksgiving* for his blessings

● *Supplication* (asking for what you need)

■ Go to your local Christian bookstore or online and find a spiritual book that touches your heart. You might start with a book by Max Lucado, whose beautiful prose puts God's love into immediate, personal context. Allow the book to speak to you of God's forgiveness, love, and mercy.

■ Consider switching to a Christian radio station or purchasing Christian music in a style you

> "BE JOYFUL IN HOPE, PATIENT IN AFFLICTION, FAITHFUL IN PRAYER."
> —ROMANS 12:12

enjoy. Listen to it in the car, at home, and at work whenever possible.

- Consider making an appointment to talk with a spiritual advisor. Be open about your depression. Pray together and seek God's wisdom and direction as you continue your recovery.

- Invite someone to lunch after services this week. Be open to God's leading as to whom that person should be. Confirm your faith with that person and be open, if it seems appropriate, about what you are going through. Pick up the check.

- Intentionally focus on God. Be aware of God's presence in your life. Call on his name throughout the day. Visualize Jesus walking with you. Invite him into your life and your thoughts. Maintain a constant sense of prayerful contact.

EVEN PAIN HAS A PURPOSE IN GOD'S PLAN.

You must want to keep going, keep growing, keep healing. I promise, if you keep working at recovery, it will come. I have seen it countless times and have witnessed the joy that comes on the other side of depression. I have seen the wisdom gained from living through this dark time of doubt and fear. You will find your way into the light again.

Even pain has a purpose in God's plan. Pain offers a deep maturity and appreciation for life. It is like climbing to the top of a great mountain, which you cannot accomplish without an arduous ascent. But sunrise at the top of the world puts all of the stumbles, aches, and pains of the climb into perspective. Recovery allows you to see your world and yourself anew.

Notes

1. Lindsey Tanner, "Treatment for Depression on the Rise," *Seattle Post-Intelligencer* (January 8, 2002). http://www.seattlepi.com/national/article/Treatment-for-depression-on-the-rise-1076817.php.

2. Robert A. Anderson, *Clinician's Guide to Holistic Medicine* (NY: MacGraw-Hill Publishing, 2001), 243.

3. R. C. W. Hall, E. R. Gardner, M. K. Popkin, and S. K. Stickney, "Unrecognized Physical Illness Prompting Psychiatric Admission: A Prospective Study," *American Journal of Psychiatry* 138, no. 5 (May 1981): 629–35.

4. I. Hickie, B. Bennet, P. Mitchell, K. Wilhelm, and W. Orlay, "Clinical and Subclinical Hypothyroidism Inpatients with Chronic and Treatment-Resistant Depression." *Australian and New Zealand Journal of Psychiatry* 30, no. 2 (1996): 246–52.

5. E. Barrett-Connor, D. G. Von Muhlen, and D. Kristz-Silverstein, "Bioavailable Testosterone and Depressed Mood in Older Men: The Rancho Bernardo Study." *Journal of Clinical Endocrinology Metabolism* 84, no. 2 (February 1999): 573–7.

6. I. R. Bell, M. L. Jasnoski, J. Kagan, and D. S. King, "Depression and Allergies: Survey of a Nonclinical Population." *Psychotherapy and Psychosomatics* 55, no.1 (1991): 24–31.

7. Carl C. Pfeiffer, *Nutrition and Mental Illness* (Rochester, Vt: Healing Arts Press, 1987).

8. M. J. Martena. J. C. Van Der Wielen, I. M. Rietjens, W. N. Klerx, H. N. De Groot, E. J. Konings. "Monitoring of Mercury, Arsenic, and Lead in Traditional Asian Herbal Preparations on the Dutch Market and Estimation of Associated Risks." Food Additives and Contaminants Part A, Chemistry, Analysis, Control, Exposure and Risk Assessment 27, no. 2 (February 2010):190–205. doi: 10.1080/02652030903207235.

9. W. J. Visser and F. L. Van de Vyver. "Aluminium-induced Osteomalacia in Severe Chronic Renal Failure (SCRF)," *Clinical Nephrology* 24, suppl. 1 (1985): S30–6.

10. Syd Baumel, *Dealing with Depression Naturally: Complementary and Alternative Therapies for Restoring Emotional Health* (Lincolnwood, IL: Keats Publishing, 1998), 27.

11. Carol Ann Turkington and Eliot F. Kaplan, *Making the Prozac Decision: A Guide to Antidepressants* (LA: Lowell House, 1997).

12. F. Dimeo, M. Bauer, I. Varahram, G. Proest, and U. Halter, "Benefits from Aerobic Exercise in Patients with Major Depression: A Pilot Study," *British Journal of Sports Medicine* 35 (April 2001):114–117.

13. "Study: Exercise Has Long-Lasting Effect on Depression," *Duke Today* (September 22, 2000). https://today.duke.edu/2000/09/exercise922.html.